THIS BOOK BELONGS TO

_____

_____

_____

Alphabet Warm Ups

Aa Aa Aa

Aa Aa Aa

Bb Bb Bb

Bb Bb Bb

Cc Cc Cc

Cc Cc Cc Cc

Dd Dd Dd

Dd Dd Dd

Ee Ee Ee

Ee Ee Ee

Ff Ff Ff

Ff Ff Ff

Gg Gg Gg

Gg Gg Gg

Hh Hh Hh

Hh Hh Hh

Ii Ii Ii Ii Ii

Ii Ii Ii Ii Ii

Jj Jj Jj Jj

Jj Jj Jj Jj

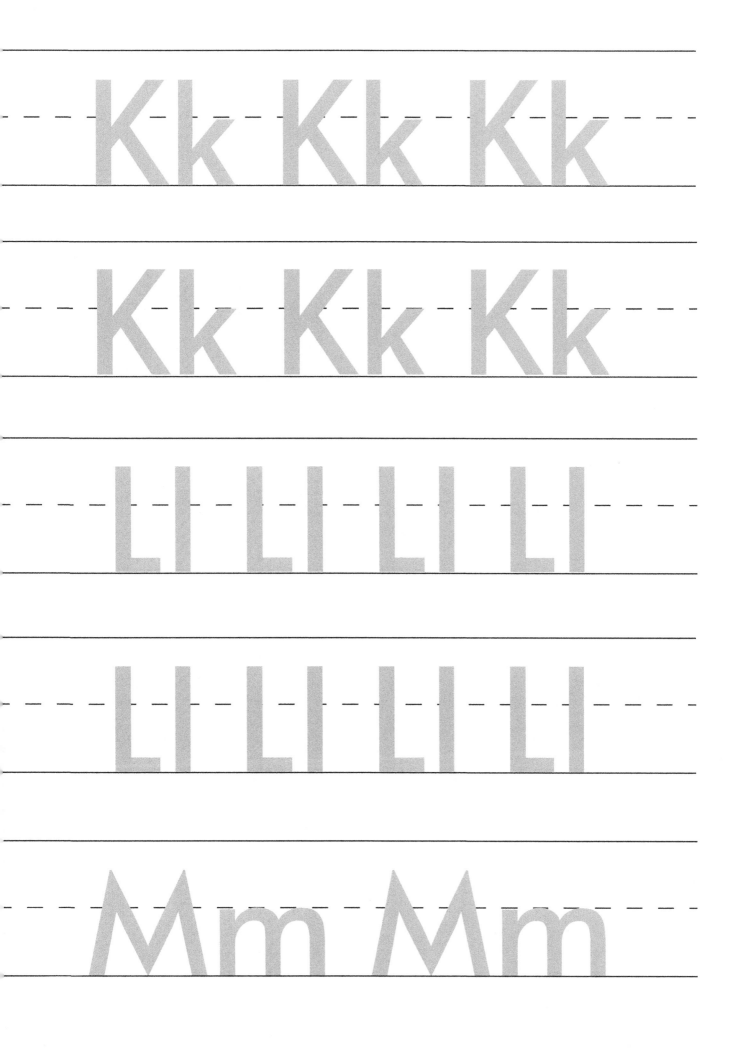

Mm Mm

Nn Nn Nn

Nn Nn Nn

Oo Oo Oo

Oo Oo Oo

Pp Pp Pp

Pp Pp Pp

Qq Qq Qq

Qq Qq Qq

Rr Rr Rr

Rr Rr Rr

Ss Ss Ss

Ss Ss Ss

Tt Tt Tt

Tt Tt Tt

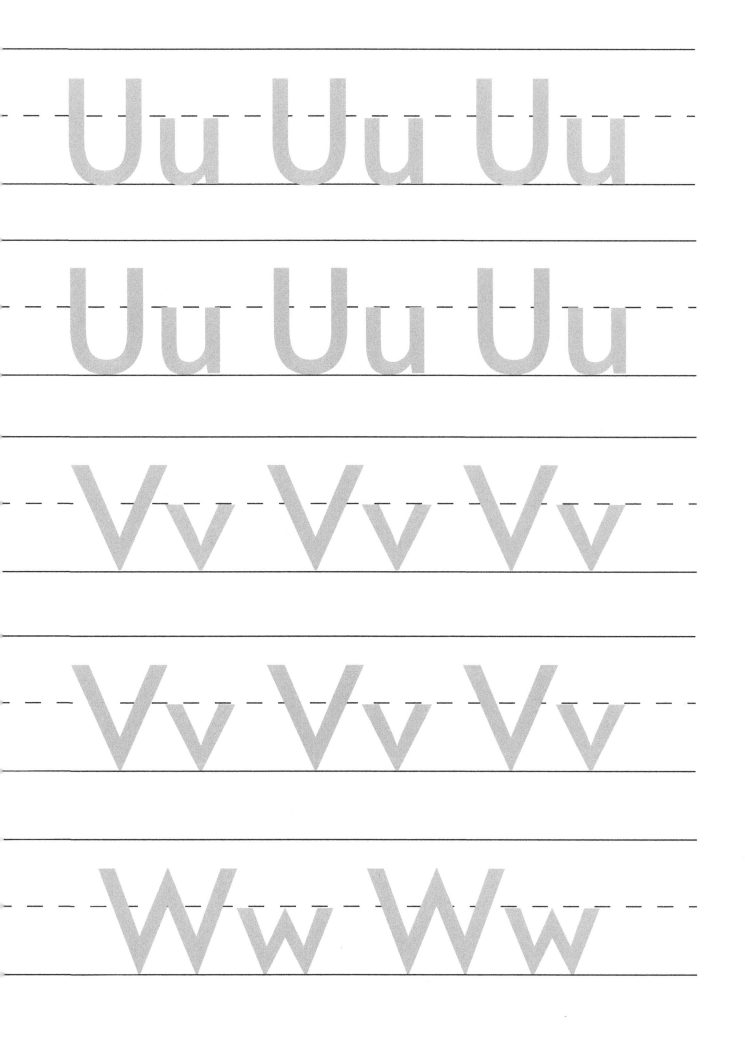

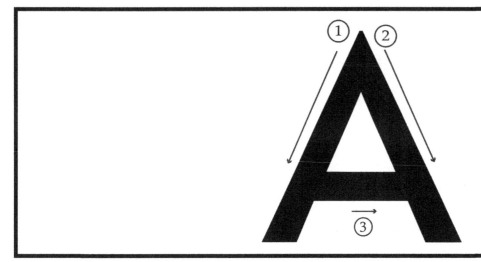

A A A A A

I had a cat.

I had a cat.

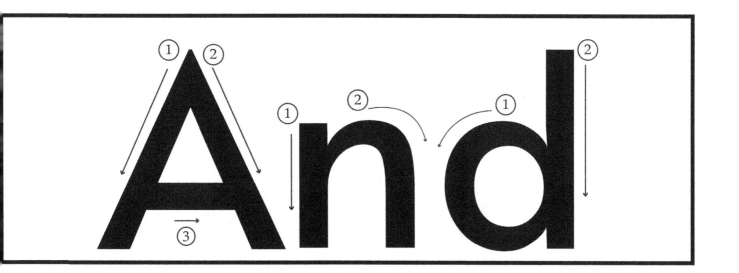

And   And   And

I like cars and trucks.

I like cars and

trucks.

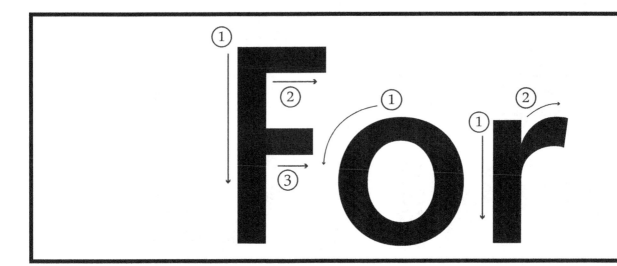

For   For   For

Fry an egg for me.

Fry an egg for

me.

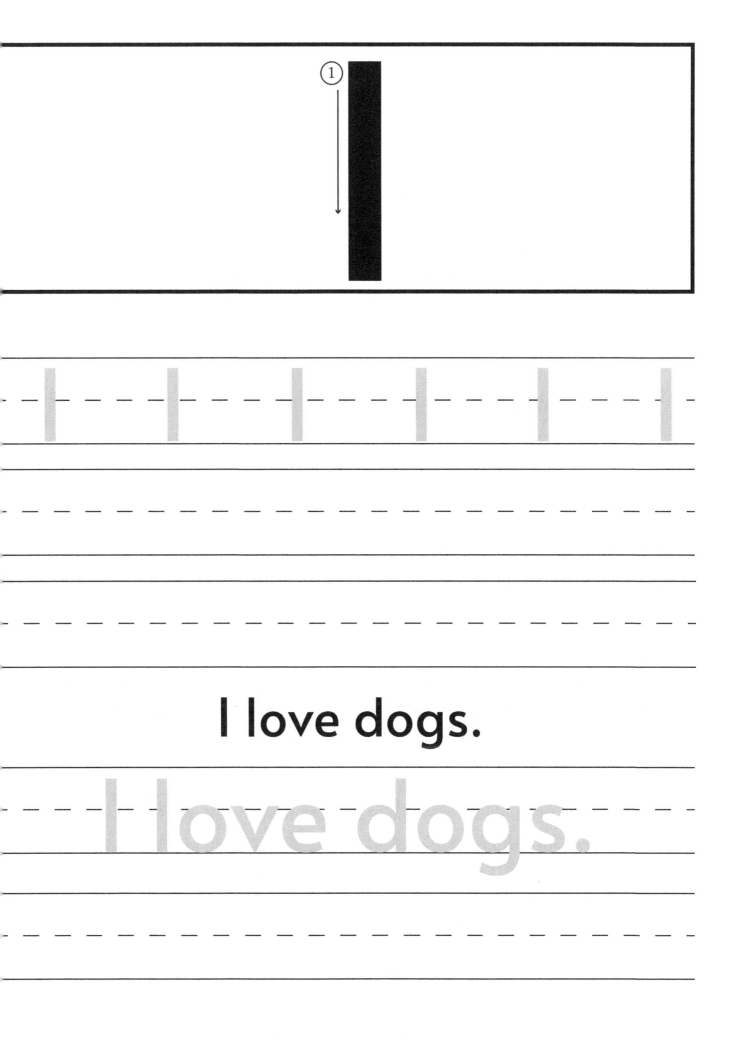

I love dogs.

I love dogs.

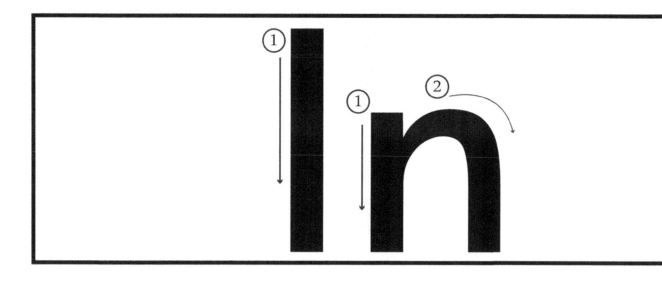

In In In In

The food is in the bag.

The food is in

the bag.

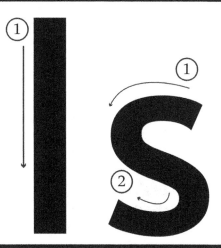

Is Is Is Is

The carrot is tasty.

The carrot is

tasty.

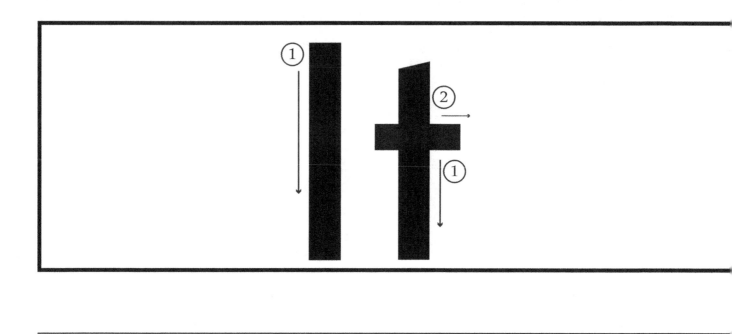

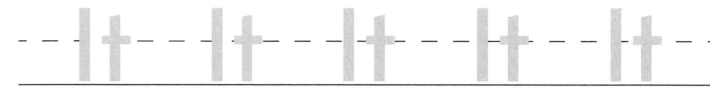

It is raining.

It is raining.

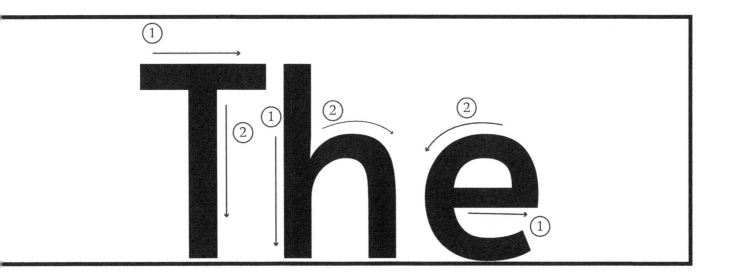

The   The   The

I fed the dog.

I fed the dog.

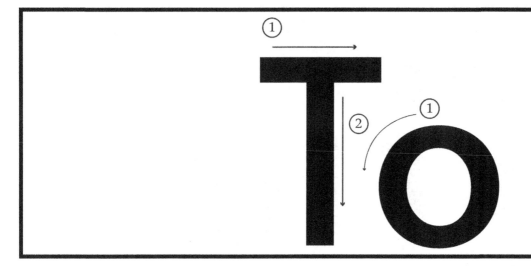

To   To   To   To

He walks to the store.

He walks to the

store.

You You You

You look happy.

You look happy.

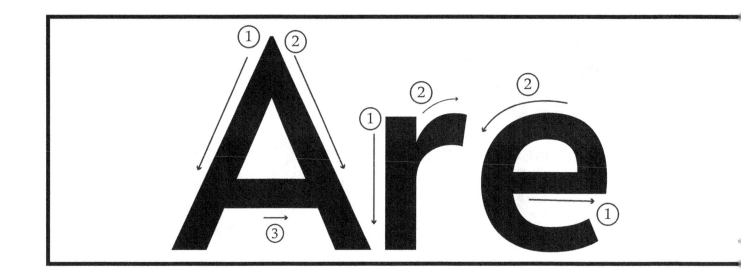

Are   Are   Are

Lemons are sour.

Lemons are

sour.

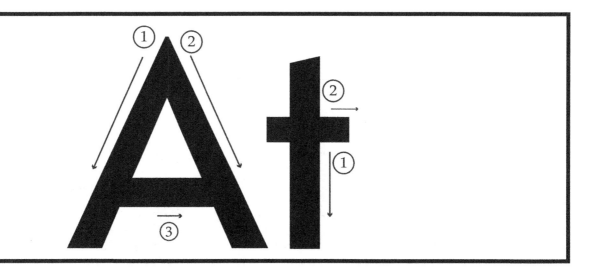

At At At At

I saw a tiger at the zoo.

I saw a tiger at the zoo.

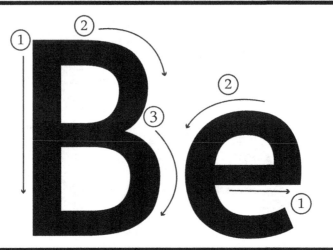

Be　Be　Be　Be

We must not be late.

We must not be

late.

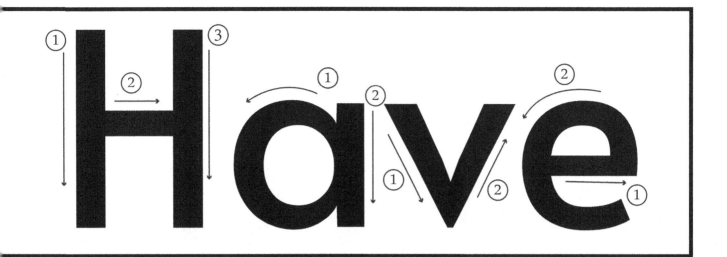

Have   Have

I have lot of story books.

I have lot of

story books.

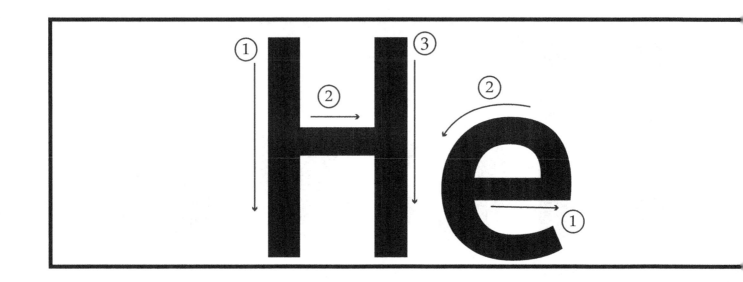

He   He   He   He

He walks to the store.

He walks to the

store.

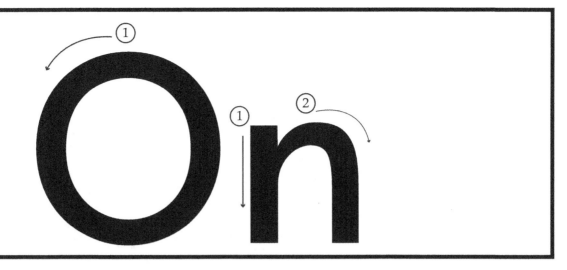

On   On   On

Put the book on the table.

Put the book on

the table.

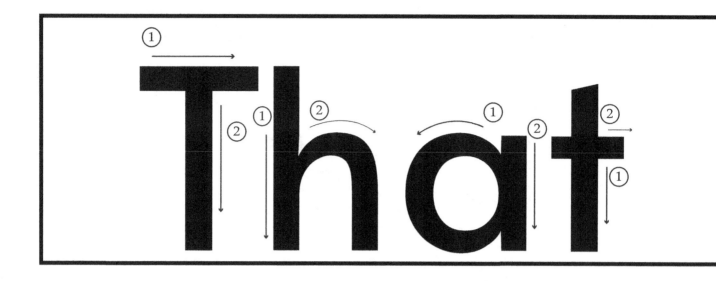

That   That

That elephant is big.

That elephant
is big.

They

They   They

They are dogs.

They are dogs.

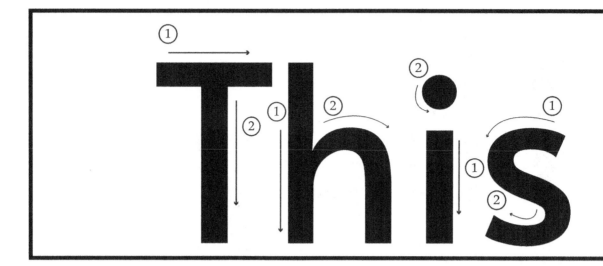

This · This · This

This is my book.

This is my book.

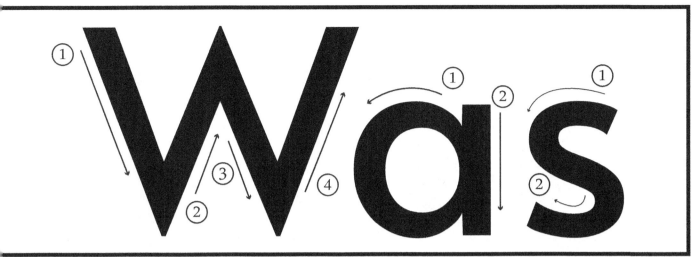

Was   Was

She was a good cat.

She was a good
cat.

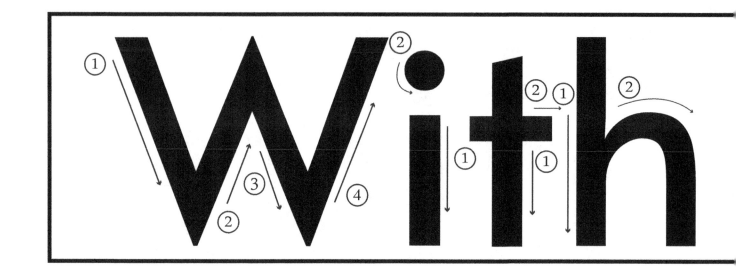

With With

He is playing with his pet.

He is playing

with his pet.

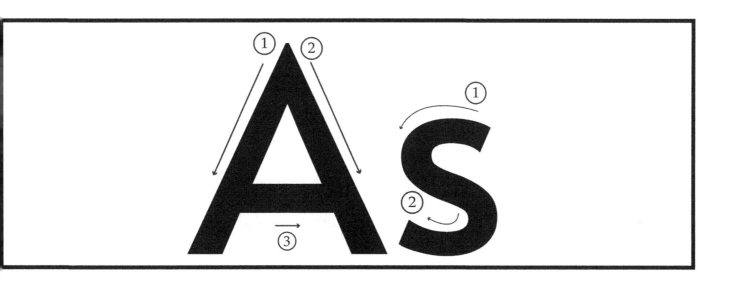

As   As   As   As

I am as fast as a rabbit.

I am as fast as
a rabbit.

From   From

I come from Boston.

I come from

Boston.

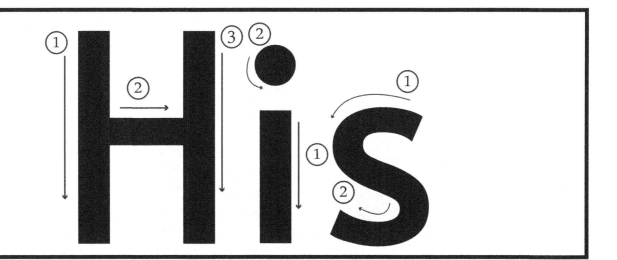

His   His   His

His car is so big.

His car is so

big.

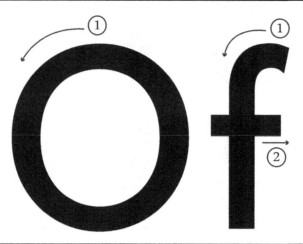

Of Of Of Of

Two of us jump.

Two of us jump.

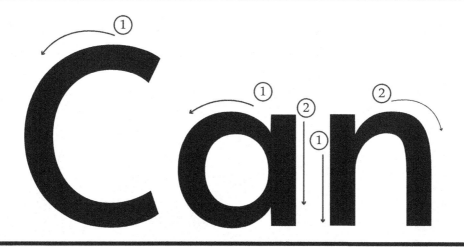

Can   Can   Can

I can read!

I can read!

Not Not Not

I did not eat lunch.

I did not eat

lunch.

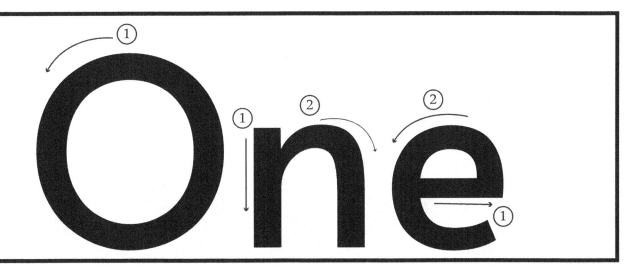

One One

I want one cookie.

I want one

cookie.

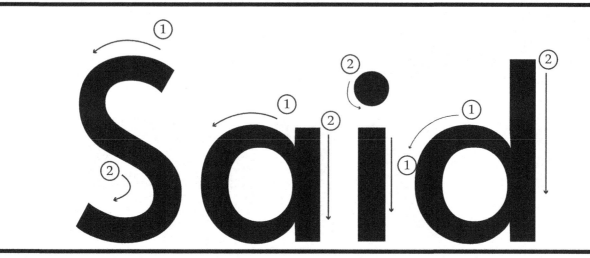

Said Said

She said goodbye.

She said

goodbye.

We   We   We

We are happy.

We are happy.

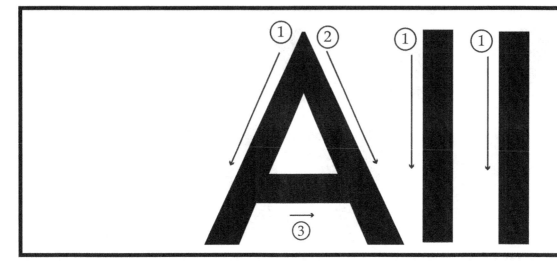

All   All   All

We all like cycling.

We all like

cycling.

But But But

Wood floats, but iron sinks.

Wood floats,

but iron sinks.

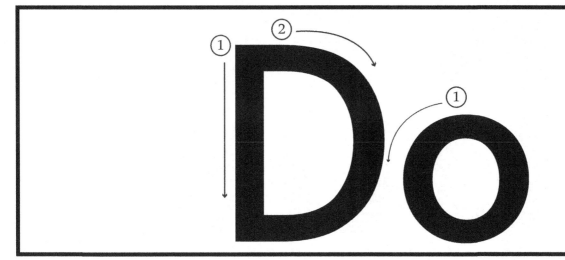

Do   Do   Do

I will do my work.

I will do my

work.

She

She She She

She has a doll.

She has a doll.

There

There   There

There is your school bag.

There is your

school bag.

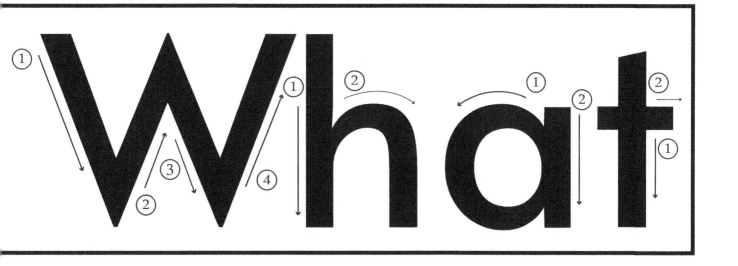

What   What

What is the story?

What is the

story?

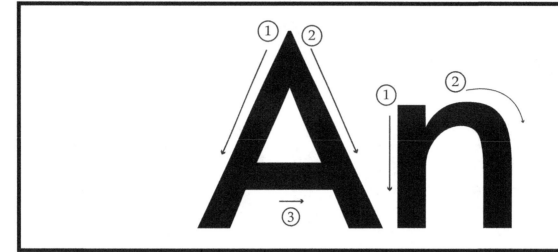

An An An

An apple is red.

An apple is red.

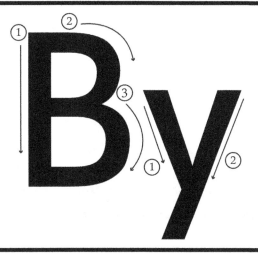

By   By   By   By

He came by bus.

He came by

bus.

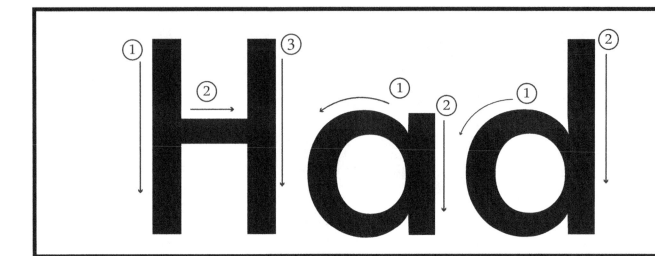

Had Had Had

We had fun today.

We had fun

today.

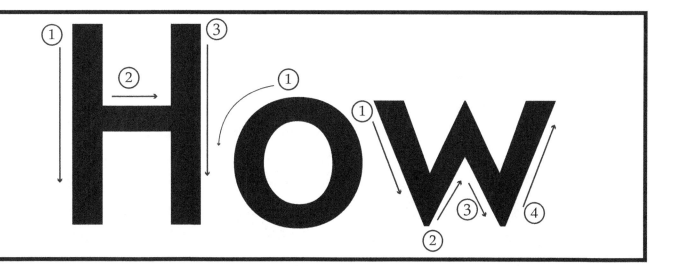

How How How

How was your summer?

How was your summer?

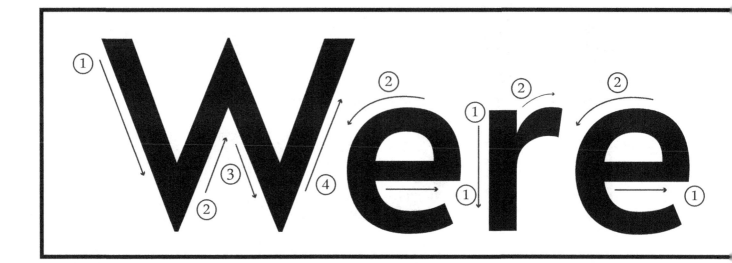

Were   Were

I wish I were rich.

I wish I were

rich.

When   When

When did you get home?

When did you

get home?

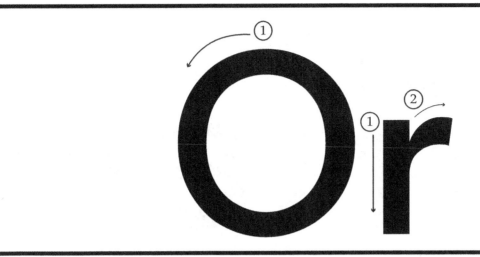

Or   Or   Or   Or

Just say yes or no.

Just say yes

or no.

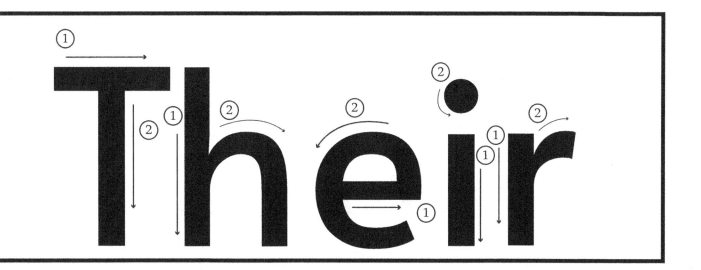

Their   Their

I like their pictures.

I like their
pictures.

Use   Use   Use

Use your key.

Use your key.

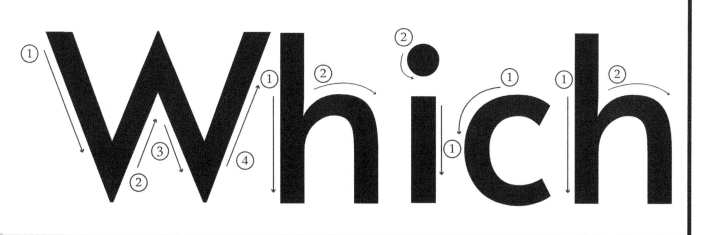

Which   Which

Which is our car?

Which is our

car?

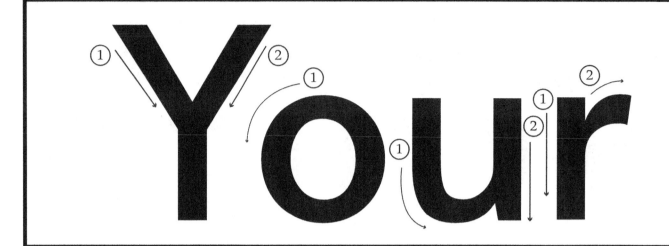

Your Your

Clean your room.

Clean your

room.

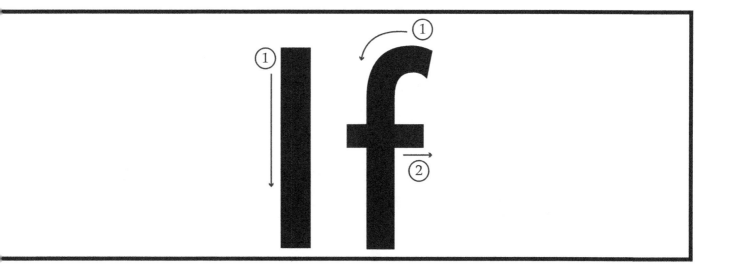

If   If   If   If   If

He acts as if he were a king.

He acts as if he

were a king.

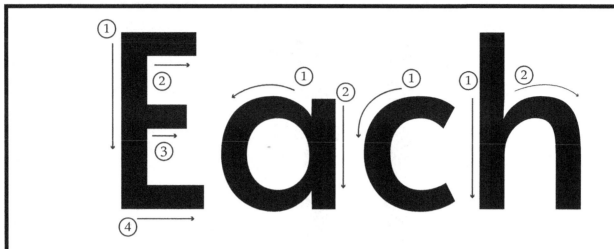

Each   Each

Each one is different.

Each one is

different.

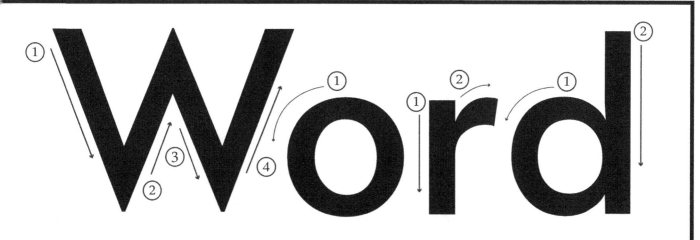

Word   Word

Every word you type.

Every word you type.

Go   Go   Go

We will go home.

We will go

home.

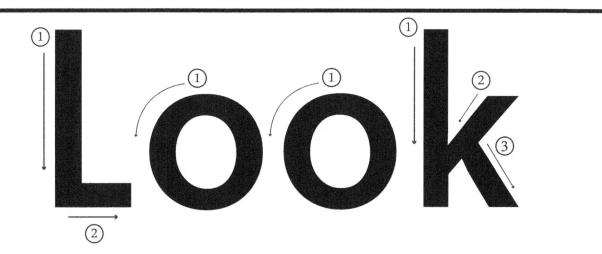

Look Look

Look at my new doll.

Look at my new

doll.

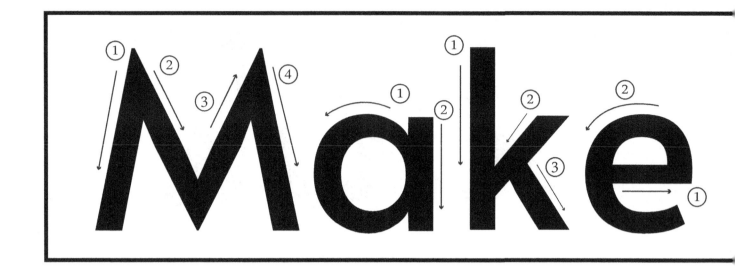

Make   Make

You make me happy.

You make me

happy.

See

See See See

I see a bird.

I see a bird.

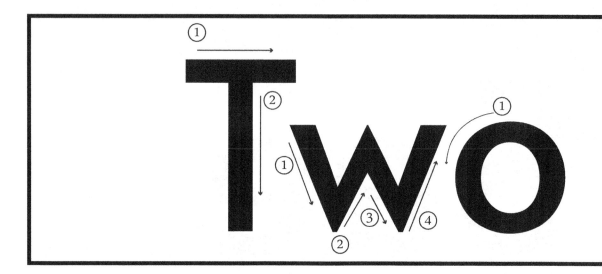

Two   Two   Two

I have two pieces of cake.

I have two

pieces of cake.

Up   Up   Up

Turn up the TV.

Turn up the TV.

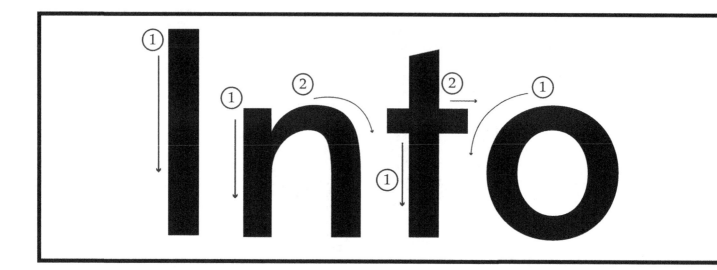

Into   Into   Into

Tom got into bed.

Tom got into

bed.

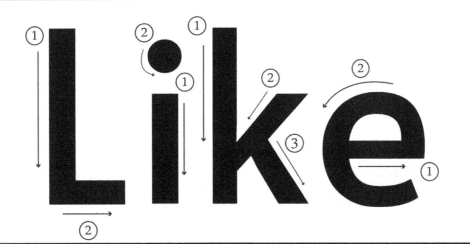

Like   Like   Like

I like cookies.

I like cookies.

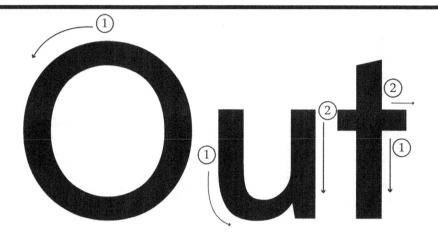

Out Out Out

He took out some coins.

He took out
some coins.

So   So   So   So

You are looking so pretty.

You are looking
so pretty.

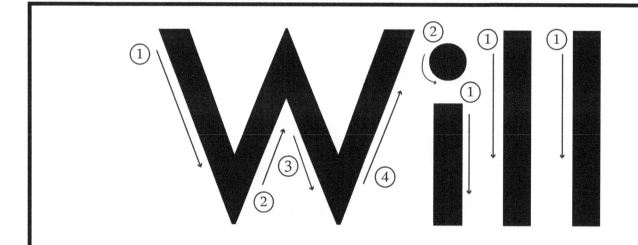

Will Will Will

I will have a cup of tea.

I will have a

cup of tea.

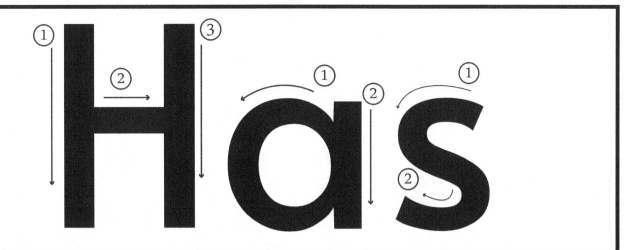

Has   Has   Has

That girl has a ball.

That girl has a

ball.

Her   Her   Her

She bought her a ring.

She bought her

a ring.

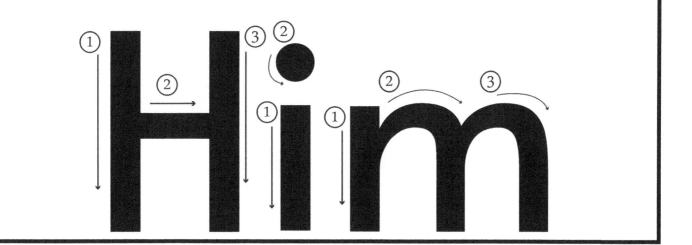

Him Him Him

She bought him a car.

She bought him
a car.

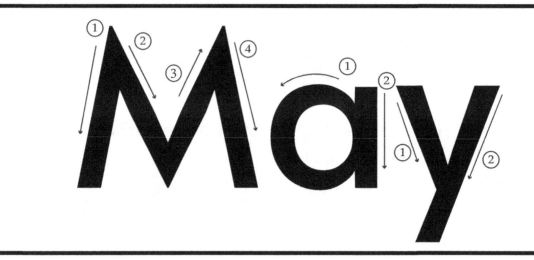

May May

May I sit here?

May I sit here?

Some

Some   Some

Give me some fruits to eat.

Give me some

fruits to eat.

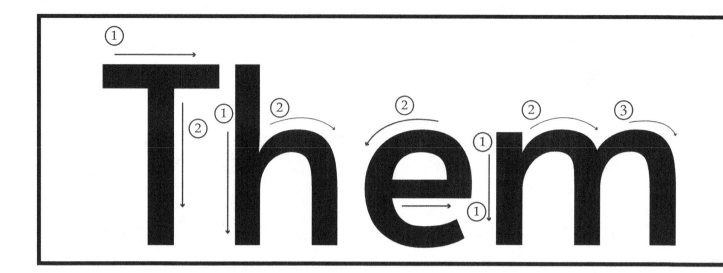

Them   Them

May I eat one of them?

May I eat one
of them?

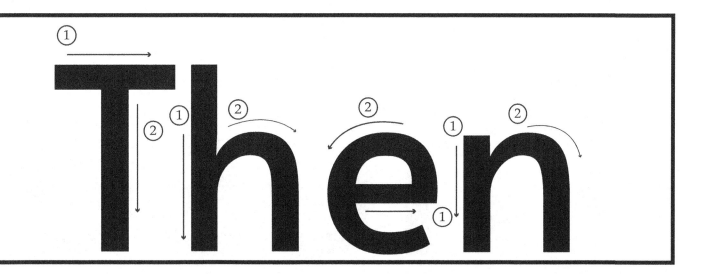

Then Then

We were younger then.

We were
younger then.

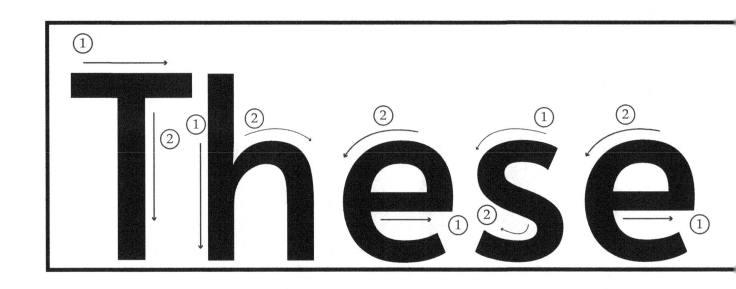

These   These

These are shoes.

These are

shoes.

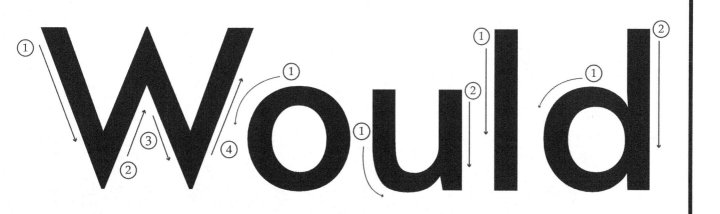

Would Would

Would you like it again?

Would you like

it again?

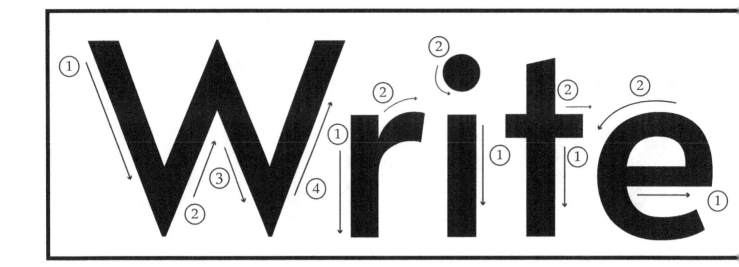

Write   Write

Write it down.

Write it down.

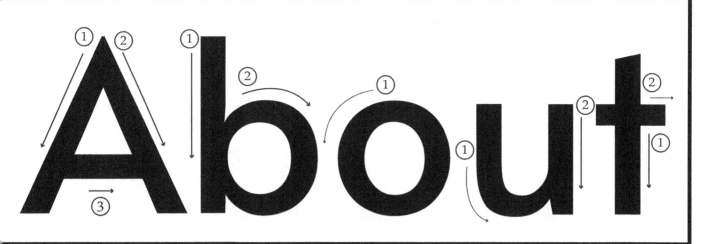

About   About

How about you?

How about

you?

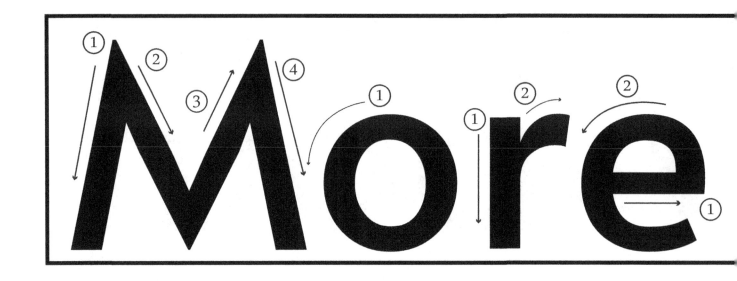

More   More

I want more milk.

I want more milk.

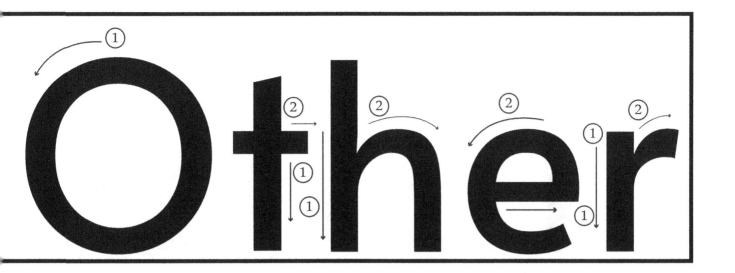

Other   Other

We know each other.

We know each

other.

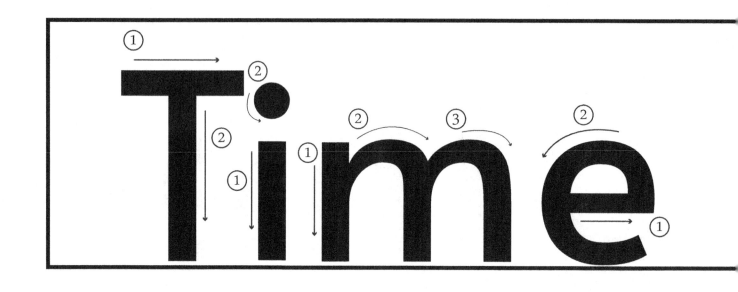

Time   Time

Take your food on time.

Take your food

on time.

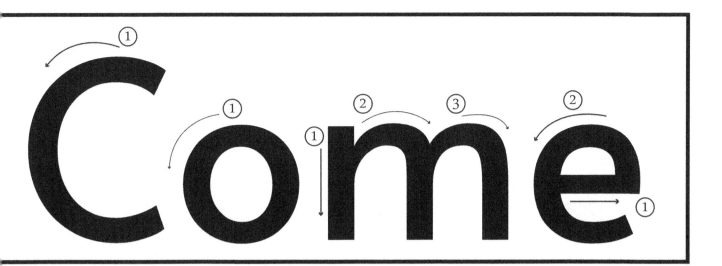

Come   Come

She will come to play.

She will come

to play.

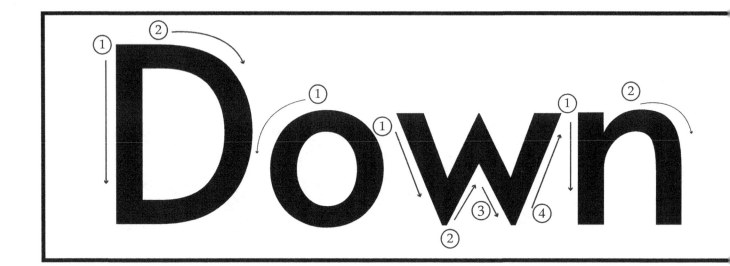

Down   Down

I am going down the stairs.

I am going

down the stairs.

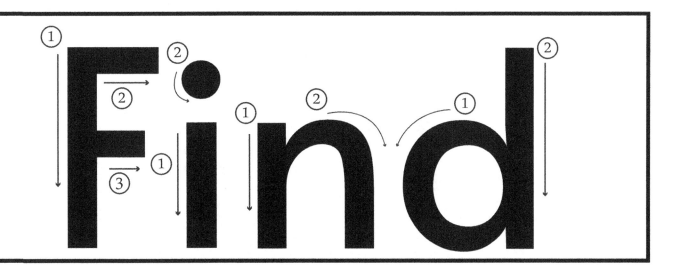

Find   Find   Find

Can you find my pencil?

Can you find

my pencil?

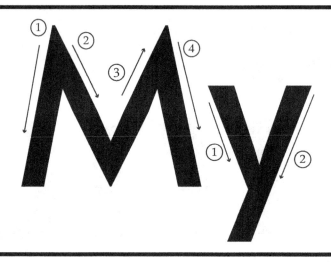

My   My   My

I love my family.

I love my

family.

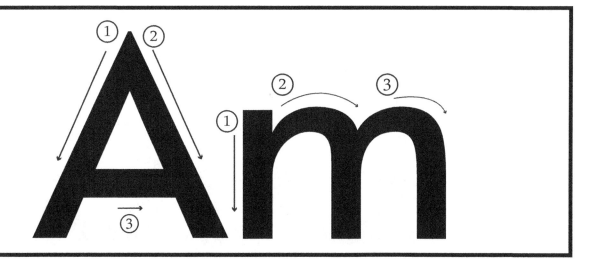

Am Am Am

I am in Kindergarten.

I am in

Kindergarten.

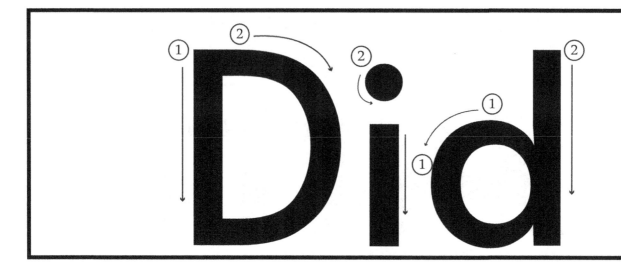

Did   Did   Did

I did not have her blue pen.

I did not have

her blue pen.

Get   Get   Get

I will get some cake.

I will get some

cake.

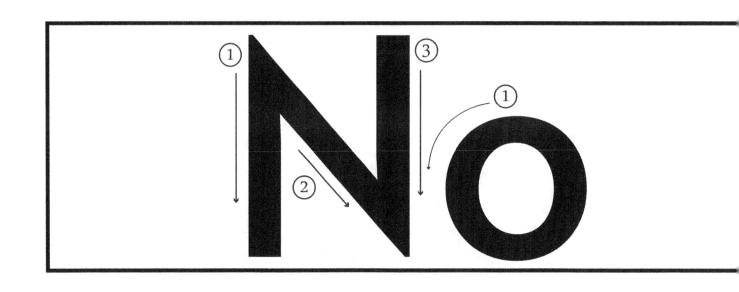

No No No

Just say no to plastic bags.

Just say no to

plastic bags.

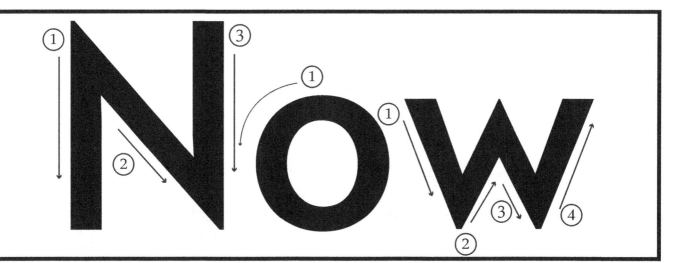

Now   Now

It is cloudy now.

It is cloudy now.

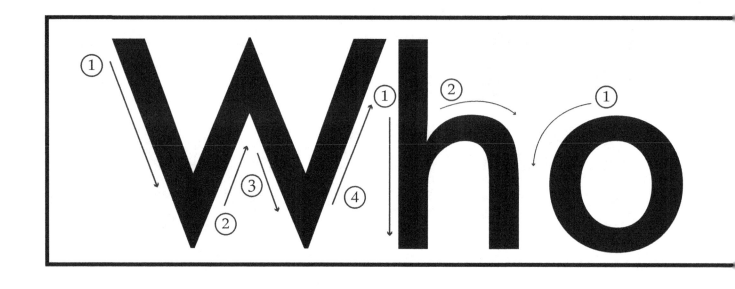

Who   Who

Who was playing?

Who was

playing?

Could   Could

I wish I could swim.

I wish I could

swim.

B e e n

Been   Been

I have never been to Paris.

I have never

been to Paris.

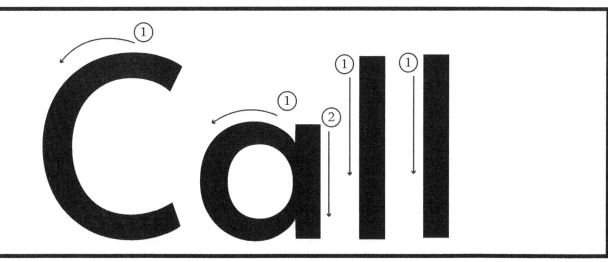

Call Call Call

Call the doctor.

Call the doctor.

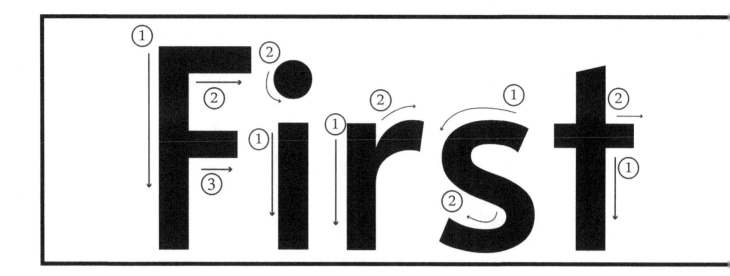

First   First   First

This is my first teddy bear.

This is my first

teddy bear.

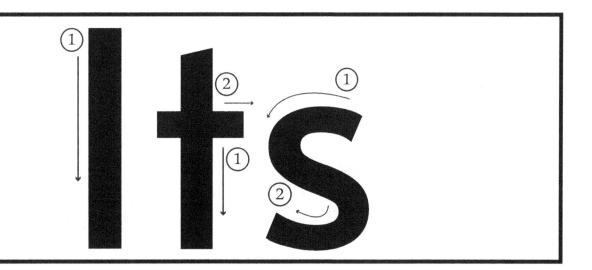

Its Its Its Its

The plant is in its pot.

The plant is in

its pot.

Made Made

She made me a cake.

She made me

a cake.

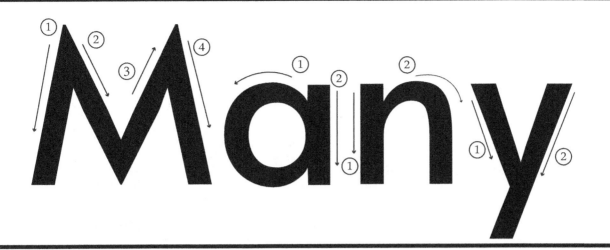

Many Many

I have many toys.

I have many
toys.

Long

Long Long

She has long hair.

She has long hair.

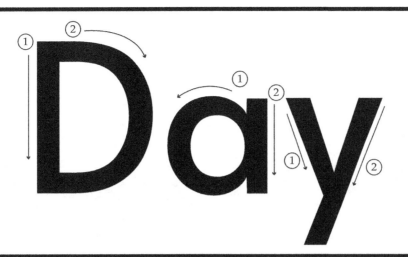

Day   Day   Day

It is a sunny day.

It is a sunny
day.

Number

Number

My lucky number is 6.

My lucky

number is 6.

Part

Part   Part   Part

He acted the part of King.

He acted the part of King.

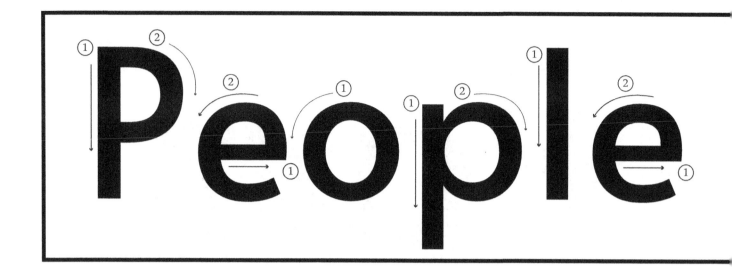

People   People

They are good people.

They are good

people.

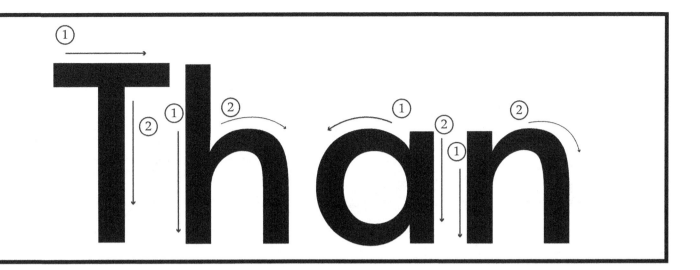

Than   Than

Tom is taller than me.

Tom is taller

than me.

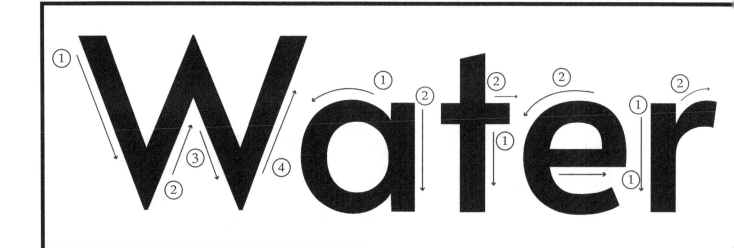

Water   Water

I need water.

I need water.

Way   Way

I know the way.

I know the way.